D1281955

DAY
SAILING

DAY SAILING

DAVID R. SLAVITT

THE UNIVERSITY OF NORTH CAROLINA PRESS
CHAPEL HILL
1969

FOR LYNN

Io mi volsi a Beatrice, e quella udìo
pria ch' io parlassi, e arrisemi un cenno
che fece crescer l' ali al voler mio.

CONTENTS

I

DAY SAILING | 3
PRECAUTIONS | 5
SESTINA FOR THE LAST WEEK OF MARCH | 7
PRUNING | 9
THE CLEARING | 10
ORLEANS WRECKERS | 11
FALL | 13
THE WEB | 14
PLYMOUTH ROCK | 15
CAPE COD HOUSE | 16
UNCLES WIGGLE THEIR EARS | 17
AUBADE | 18
SUMMER SHOWER | 19
SEALS | 20
HARBOR | 22
THREE IDEAS OF DISORDER | 23
    I. THE WHALES
    II. BUILDING, PLANTING, ETC.
    III. THE POND

II

LUTE | 29
SWOBODA | 30
LEPORELLO, IN HIS DRESSING ROOM | 31
THE DEATH OF MOZART | 32
THREE LOVE POEMS | 33
COMPLIMENT UPON A LAUGH | 35
TABLEAU A LA ROUSSEAU | 36
SAPPHIC FRAGMENTS | 37
DIALOGUE IN ITHAKA | 38
UPON RECEIVING A BOOK OF POEMS | 39
IMPROVISATION ON THEMES OF JOHN DONNE | 40
EPITAPH FOR GOLIATH | 41
PROLEGOMENON TO THE STUDY OF POETICS | 42

GREAT CIRCLE ROUTE | 43
CASTELLO SFORZESCO | 44
BATH | 45
HELLBRUNN | 47
A RONDELET FROM A FRAGMENT OF ARCHILOCHUS | 49
A TRIOLET FROM ANOTHER FRAGMENT | 50
GALLUS (AFTER ECLOGA X) | 51

III
ANOTHER LETTER TO LORD BYRON | 55

IV
EXHORTATION TO AN ARAB FRIEND (1965) | 61
JONAH: A REPORT | 64
THE COVENANT | 67
PROLOGUE TO A PLAY: SAMUEL SPEAKS | 68
A GARLAND FOR ST. AGNES ON MY BIRTHDAY | 69

I

DAY SAILING

1.

Distance deceives. Novelists mistake
extent for weight, their thicknesses
for acuity. Endurance rarely
endures. Chichester, Bannister,
Sisyphus sweat. Lazier,
I cannot believe that far,
go to no such lengths.
Day sailing in a small catboat in the bay
satisfies me, who have nowhere to go.

What rarity have the Indies now
but famine, cholera and war,
what riches for a new Magellan
or Drake to take from that arduous route?
The Pacific boils with testing;
Atlantis is long sunk.

Still, the mainsheet tugs,
tiller and centerboard purr.
The wind blows the hair.

I go sailing.

2.

It is conversation of craft and force,
the wind so, and the sail and rudder so;

it is compromise between the wind
and me, a settling for that bluff, that flagpole,
and tacking back, beating up the wind,
achieving direction out of indirection;

it is balancing, my weight
to windward, heeling to leeward;

it is a triumph, for civilization is
neither writing, nor painting pictures, nor forging metal,

nor breeding animals, nor sowing grain,
but sailing into the wind, sailing to westward,
the knowing, the craft.

The cove at low tide
swarms, gulls and terns,
sandpipers, and crows
pick over the shingle,
small crabs start,
clams squirt, worms
snake in the rich reek
of sea-wrack rot.
The muck smacks soles,
oozes between my toes.

I bring to the hull a cloth, a plank, a stick,
and bring the hull to life, and it brings me
off the shingle, into the narrow channel,
and out into the bay. The fetor fades
to salt. The wind freshens.

I have my craft—a skill, a trade, duplicity,
a small boat.

3.
The intricate maneuvering for the sake
of maneuvering, or to put myself in the sun
for my tan, or out of the sun for fear of burn,
or just to adjust the look of the boat is not
different from our comfortable lives ashore,
neither praiseworthy nor blameworthy,
except that sometimes when a fresh wind comes up
out of nowhere, out of the south, and I
have to head south to the cove, and the spray breaks
over the bow, and the boat slants, riding, riving
the water, comes about sharp, smart, to find
that it is, I am, seaworthy is something.
I am no sailor, but there is no virtue
wholly irrelevant. The seaman with the oar
must find the farmer willing to improvise
some use for what he carries, able to see
it could make do, perhaps, as a winnowing fan.

PRECAUTIONS

The twin red pennants of gale warnings drooped
in the dead calm air. Alma, the radio said,
was off Atlantic City: still, the harbor
was still and the air. A mosquito looped
in triumph over the wind of his small will
in virtuoso passes about my head.
I hauled the boat ashore. It was heavy labor.
My boots were heavy. Everything was still
as an impasto landscape not yet dry,
or, if reports be true, as Alma's eye.

I stripped the boat, carried the spars to a bluff
above the reach of any tide. Their varnish
soaked up the sun like syrup, and the sweat
poured down my back like syrup. Good enough.
I dug the anchor into the mud and left
the storm to do its worst, thinking the swinish
weekenders whose boats rode light would get
the wrecks they deserved, spars snapped, their craft adrift
in gale force winds to founder. I drove home
to wait for the weather reports, and the weather to come.

That night it rained some, and the wind rose
but only a little. Eight on the black nine,
and still no storm, or storm but out to sea.
Seven on the eight. I went to bed. All those
boats of the careless weekenders survived
an ordinary night. Battered to bits
they should have been, all wrecked, and only mine
secure in a just world. At Nineveh, He
juggled with gourds for Jonah, but what the hell
difference does anything make if all ends well?

Take Noah, with the ark all built, the hold
an incredible zoo, waiting, waiting for rain
which is predicted but never quite appears
and instead follows a low pressure trough, or a cold
front to the Persian Gulf. Or take Lot,
packing, quitting the cities of the plain
to which nothing at all happens. The careers

5

of these men are dreadful—rage at the world for not
ending at noon for its wickedness as it should.
The wicked are comforted. It corrupts the good.

There's no sense to it. I remember a tree,
a dead pine that a gust of wind blew over
and the way it hit, just a few feet away
from my children. It was out of sight of the sea
but it was the same wind, the same whim
of the wind, and we could feel the earth quiver
as if it were water. The children stopped their play
a moment, then balanced, danced upon the grim
dead threat, delighted. Lord, let me
keep that balance, that equanimity.

SESTINA FOR THE LAST WEEK OF MARCH

Suddenly the ground is flesh and yielding
as if one walked on a body, and air is breath
and the woods are full of delicate, naked ladies
who hide in bushes and beckon behind the trees
in all the tempting attitudes of abandon
of the famous streets of certain infamous cities.

Who has not heard the erotic promise of cities,
or walked in squares with the light abruptly yielding
to shadows of unimaginable abandon?
But here, in the daylight and fresh air, the breath
of gin hangs on the juniper, and trees
carefully pose themselves like elegant ladies

considering some indiscretion. Ladies
learn to conceal such thoughts in civilized cities.
Oh, sometimes, in a formal park, the trees
will make their improper suggestions, conversation yielding
to difficult silences, the very drawing of breath
becoming absurdly physical: "Abandon

pretense, civilization, cities. Abandon
all the constraints by which you live as ladies.
Strip naked, lie in the grass, pick baby's-breath
bouquets, and flee for your lives, flee the cities . . ."
But they never do. That week of spring yielding
yields itself to summer. Leaves clothe the trees.

And yet, some must have gone. Behind the trees,
those delicate creatures of our fancy's abandon
must have begun somewhere. There are myths yielding
many examples—reasonable ladies
of the kind one meets in fashionable cities
once, in the woods, struggled to catch their breath

and changed in the time it takes to draw a breath,
turning into, melting into trees.
Their stories are embroidered back in the cities,

tamed for us who can bear only so much abandon.
They have been refined, no doubt for the sake of the ladies
who know their truth and long for such a yielding

and for gentlemen of the cities, lest they abandon
fine careers, fine ladies, and run off, yielding
to the whispered breath of nymphs, behind the trees.

PRUNING

If Aphrodite poured the oil of roses
upon dead Hector and over all love, all war,
the spring still brings new eyes, the new leaf buds,
and even to the oldest bush the pruner
must come to thin, to cut back, to make way.
Romaunt, war, tautology, and all
the other roses, yet is a rose compost,
bone meal or hoof-and-horn, and sand, for drainage,
but mainly pruning, cutting back old runners
to channel the sap into the new wood
abundantly for blooms worth all that labor.
And so the idea of roses, to let the children
cut roses for their mother, tend the seedlings,
eat rose hips, taste the fruit, and learn to tell
the Grand'mere Jennies from the Buccaneers,
and, knowing the bush before the burning, read
with prickered fingers some of the rose's poems.

THE CLEARING

The sky clears, as slate shatters
and light pours, sky blue,
through the gray shards, or melts or tatters,
or merely pales. It is anyway too
dramatic, silly, as the rube's rustic
grin, looking up. What does he know?
As much as the city boy, the mystic
faker, the windowbox Wordsworth. No,
it doesn't, it doesn't mean a thing,
no more than dawn does and the east
all lit with pink, or the coming of spring
and the brown gone green. Let us at least
admit to having been up in a plane,
having seen, from the porthole, cloud banks under
which there was in one place rain
and, in another, sunlight. The wonder
is not that a sky should clear, but that we
should still feel, who know these things,
that hope dawns with dawns. It's perversity,
finding life in clearings, in springs.
It's Pavlov and Jung, joking together.

The light returns. Up go the eyes
in silent prayer to a change of weather,
and, if there's any sense, he dies,
right then. Out. And ought to go.
But what does it matter? Let light come
and, vegetables, we start to grow.
Our hearts, like vegetables, are dumb.

ORLEANS WRECKERS

New Bedford's whales were but small fry to these
fishers of men. They hung their hopes in trees,
lights in the darkness, steady or flashing beacons
on moonless nights. It was kindness of a kind,
when waves beat on the shore. Sometimes in a storm
even the sea gets seasick, water weakens,
and wants to come inland to dry. On elm or pine,
a lamp or two hung right worked like a charm.
The channels at least could come up with the wreckers
and from the beach peer back out at the breakers.

Off shore, the captains steered between the grief
of wreckers' lights and that of disbelief
in every light on the chart. (The old chaos
before the seas and firmament were first
torn apart at the break of the third day
seeps back. The Red Sea miracle surely cost
something: think of the miracle reversed
and Israel under sail.) Their ships made way
or drifted as rocks flirted with oak ribs,
and the wreckers watched like spiders in their webs.

But it was worse than that. Imagine flies,
caught and killed, that turn into allies
of the spider and sing like sirens to their brothers.
To the rocks, the tide, the lying lights, add wrecks
of merchantmen that had gone down before,
their hulls new hazards now for all the others.
Drowned masters on their slimy quarterdecks
connived with their new partners on the shore
to ply the salvage trade. About their hulls
they improvised their own crossed bones and skulls.

They have taken over the business, and from the grave
still take ships, salvage cargos and still save
sailors from the weather. Their wrecks are charted
and marked by the Coast Guard. The bell buoys toll
like steeples of whole churches that have gone down,

which is what they want — to finish what they started,
send back the tides from the bottom up over the shoal,
past sandbar, beach, and up into the town
till the channel they tried for runs along Main Street.
And the Cape is losing ground: each year, four feet.

FALL

It must have been this time of year,
mid-September, when apples fall
from the lower boughs of apple trees—
which is reasonable. In the queer
gardens the painters imagine, all
the plants bloom and bear what they please.
The only rule is for large leaves
to cover Adam's loins and Eve's.

But apples ripen now, and as
they ate they may have wondered why
those bottom leaves on the elm had turned
yellow while the maple was
redder than usual. Still, the sky
was its normal blue, and if they discerned
that the nights had seemed perhaps less warm
than previously, they saw no harm.

Often the painters' angels hold
their burning swords aloft in "The Fall
from Grace," or some such title. But
it was worse than that. It just got cold,
the leaves fell off the trees and all
the naked branches pointed at
the naked pair who knew no reason
for the change of mood, the change of season.

What angel could terrify like an oak,
so familiar a tree gone bright with so
abrupt a show of crimson? How
much worse than the obvious thunderstroke
was the quiet indictment of the snow
of their nakedness! We are used to it now,
and only inaccurate painters remember
how we thought before that first September.

THE WEB

It was not the struggle against those sticky meshes,
the futile flutter of wings of that brown moth,
nor the dark spider in the corner of the web,
watching its dinner, nor even the whole performance
between the window pane and window screen
of the old melodrama, but my daughter,
her eyes stuck to that web and her mind caught,
spun out between the twitch of those delicate wings
and the dance of approach of the spider's precise feet.
I watched her study it. And you watched me.
What a web of attention, spun from what
far beams, in that intricate polygon!
Innocent, we fly into these things.

The spider killed the moth. She turned away.
I turned to you, and saw your smile's trace
in the light there, faint lines around the mouth,
like those still quivering lines. What intricate
polygons, spun from what far beams!

PLYMOUTH ROCK

Across from a Howard Johnson's and down the street
from Standish Chevrolet, it's there, all right,
that rock on which presumably Pilgrim feet
first hopped from the deck of the Mayflower—a sight
to see, or the rock is, anyway. What heart
but beats a little faster for the start
of something? And all the school books teach
that this was where it began. So tourists come,
not knowing a thing about First Encounter Beach
across the bay, and stare for a while, dumb

with awe, or guilt at its absence, and then get
window or bumper stickers, souvenirs
of their own pilgrimages. And why not forget
about that other landing and fight? It appears
persnickety for a history to begin
with a battle the founding fathers didn't win.
The Indians drove them off easily, and they fled
here, settled here, stayed—which is the point
that Jamestown missed, not to mention Eric the Red,
or the Portugese fishermen, running their honky-tonk joint

on the Truro dunes. That story is suppressed
because we prefer to derive from the rock its gray
certainties than to romp on the sand. Half-dressed
little sailors and whores in the school's Thanksgiving play
wouldn't be right. Let them be puritan
Aldens and Standishes. Bury it all again
like the dead fish in the maize hole—Squanto's trick.
It's good for growth. Turn over the rock now
and God knows what crawly things would make us sick
wriggling out in the light. But I wonder how

it really happened, whether there was a fight
at First Encounter Beach, or Bradford's men
just marched across the Cape, saw a gleam of light,
called out, ran toward it, and discovered the Portugese den
of iniquity: no Indians but whores
who packed up their pillows and sailed back to the Azores
while the Pilgrims sailed the other way—for each
must have terrified the other. The Pilgrims won—
by default, but they won. And on the Truro beach
in the summer now psychiatrists take the sun.

CAPE COD HOUSE

The builder of this room who had a sense
of grace and gave more than a thought to grandeur,
in the doors' and windows' classic pediments
and mouldings of leaves the local plasterer
could hardly have managed, is nearly a century gone,
and all his line is gone. I watch the sun
lower along their lawn, while two quail feed,
peck over the mown grass, theirs and mine.
The sun, red as the legal seal on a deed
at the day's closing, sets on the dotted line.

At night it is easier. Each piece of furniture
I lived with before stakes claim to its corner;
they signal familiarity with each other
while I eavesdrop. I am the silent partner.
I have taken title, but have not taken root,
and am taking over, learning foot by foot
to feel the space of the house as a blind man, coming
into a new room, inclines his face
to listen to walls. I study the quirks of the plumbing,
the moods of the shrubs. My nerve endings replace

the cobwebs I knocked down. It grows on me,
takes purchase of my senses. I assume
the scale and line of the house, and of Benjamin Bee,
draftsman and first occupant of this room.
I am his creature, and even know his creator—
some architect in the South whom the Civil War
impressed upon this captivated Yankee.
And so on back, until I understand
what bothered Blake who, though rebelliously,
drew how the calipers melt into God's hand.

UNCLES WIGGLE THEIR EARS

Uncles wiggle their ears and then
nieces screw up their faces to find
those nerves. We laugh, watch the dog perk
one ear as no uncle can.
Try it, stupid. Smart, the mind
will turn away from what won't work.

For six months, every day, I stood
in a lake, ass-deep, with a paralyzed
dog in my arms to pyramid
on that swimming reflex until she could
work her hind legs, and was surprised
that she learned to stand, to walk. She did,

and I suppose with the right kind of deal,
big money up front, some son of a bitch
would teach himself by continual trying
to perk one ear. I try to feel
again, to produce that first little twitch,
can't tell if it's dead or only dying.

Music: sting. And the muse becomes
Sister Kenny. In montage, show
small things growing, green and blurry.
Cut to: Stockholm. A chorus hums
(voice over). You like it? It'll go!
Can the ear come back? I try. I worry.

AUBADE

With the chirp of a rusty block
on which he pulls the light
up in the east, a gray
catbird balances day
in air that still smells of night
and a sky that is pinkish-black.

The night hunters quit and the new
hunters of day come on duty.
I turn in bed, too weary
to correct the irrelevant, cheery
birds who debate on the beauty
of niello against ormolu.

SUMMER SHOWER

*Service is supplied subject to company's terms and
conditions—copy available on request . . .*
                    —CAPE AND VINEYARD ELECTRIC CO.

A broken sign, the sky
flickered the east with lightning
and we drove east. Raindrops
spotted, spattered the windshield.
Squeal with joy at the jagged
streaks in the sky, like movies,
like comics, like the idea of
lightning!
              Oh, but children
tire of everything. Squeezing
their little interest dry,
they counted flashes, reading
the heavens' meters. The storm
lasted a short while,
but like the gods themselves,
they had long lost count.

SEALS

The fish
that fly,
dead, flung by
the counting keeper—
more to the sluggish,
fewer to the sleeker
seals—nourish
fairly, filling up
as heaven equally fills
every unequal cup.

To watch
among
them, to favor young
or elderly or sick
seals not up to catching
lunch with a trick
or to fend off the snatching
of the greedier ones requires
a number of different skills
from those the crowd admires.

And so
with seals:
youngsters take meals
in small, separate pools
where keepers throw
smelts, seal schools
where the young grow
clever, and able to compete
with adults for the flung
fish they will have to eat.

To live
in zoos,
the animals lose
natural seal sense,
and being captive,
acquire dependence,
even on imitative

children who throw balls.
The seals oblige and catch
what miscellany falls.

They bark
as they
always do, play
for a while longer,
having made of life a lark
and a game of hunger.
But later, in the dark
a seal will get sick,
get sick to death, fed up
at last with its one trick.

HARBOR

O navis, referent in mare te novi
fluctus. O quid agis! fortiter occupa portum.
—HORACE

Around the point are shallows, the treacherous
sand bars, crazy currents, attention, tense
peering for the channel, gradations in color of the water,
the look of waves, and the easy breath at the mouth
of the harbor, the turning, out of the wind
                                        and into
the look of the city, the rose walls washed
by the late sun, the lines, the roofs' gleaming.
Phoenecians on those fragile craft with sails
like trailing wings and hulls like *gondole*
must have seen cities in such a light, the sea
after, shore forward, promising tavernas
and the back street excitements of civilization.

It must be the light, the late wash of the darkening
roses, that corrupts, makes our ports like Tarsus,
like Ephesus, the end of the world seem hours
off at best, and nothing to do for the time
but pass it in a congenial way. And it passes,
and the walls, the beautiful pastel walls, fall
black into the black as black as the wind
keening out there on the spray at the point which
is the end of the world and only waits
to boil in, wash up everything, take all.

THREE IDEAS OF DISORDER

> ". . . on the other hand, we must resist the temptation
> to get off cheaply by overusing or otherwise abusing
> Rationality of Irrationality strategies."
> —HERMAN KAHN

I. THE WHALES

The whales are in the sound, and sound
of rifle fire as they blow.
Through our opened windows we see no
ragged partisans, gorgeous militiamen, in town,
nothing but morning fog infiltrating darkness. Out
beyond cove and jetty, the whales spout,
a dozen, a score, more, making a noise
of soldiers, of playing at soldiers like small boys.
Still, we are right
to feel the fear, start from our soft sleep,
and stare out toward their noises in the night,
for they are killer whales. They tear and feed
in unimaginable silence, down deep
where the bland green waves above them show
no discoloration, though
their victims bleed and bleed.
Such are the proprieties they keep.

II. BUILDING, PLANTING, ETC.

Hegel, Hegel, after the tall towers
four blocks high, or ten, after the oblong
balanced buildings, my son has learned the tough
tyranny of blocks. I have watched him struggle
against the lure of symmetry to make
a perfectly stupid building, lovably
unlovely, all projections and truncations,
a mess, splendid and functionless, and have
myself snuck into the playroom, stooped to make
an architectural monster of some kind,
but the irresistible gravity of the blocks
piles up, shows strengths, sensible lines of force.

Alaric entered Rome, you know, determined
to knock it down, knock it all down,
and not just the city either but the empire,
turning it into a tantrum, a rumpus, a pampas . . .
It made no difference. The administrative machine
of undersecretaries and junior clerks
kept on, like the hair and nails of a dead man.

It's hard to do. Bakunin said the urge
to destroy is also a creative urge. It's hard.

Do you know how to plant hyacinth bulbs and jonquils,
the only sane way to get them not
in those arbitrary rows, not in patterns,
not in any order, but perfectly stupid
and natural as flowers ought to be?
Close your eyes, throw, and where they land,
dig.

III. THE POND
The pond is blind. Spring-fed, it goes nowhere
but up and out and into the sun and air.
There are fish in it, but nobody knows how the devil
they got there. It must have connected once with something,
but there's no other water for miles. Alone, odd,
bubbling up of itself and self-containing,
it adorns the pine woods like a jewel in the navel
of a sleeping dancer, or the forehead of a god.
The trees shield it from the winds as if they were fond
of it or their own reflections in the pond.

It isn't at any rate a place where one
would expect to find anything like an abandoned gun,
but there it was, down in the black ooze
of the bottom. Politely, the algae had tried to hide
that glinting of cheap nickel-plate which shone
still, like the cheap questions: Who fired? Who died?
Somebody must have died. You don't just lose
a thirty-two that way, on a pond, alone.
We hefted the gun that someone must have hurled
here, hoping it was the deepest pond in the world.

Deep? In the middle, sixty feet, which is less
than they used to think, imagining bottomlessness
in these little ponds that glaciers scooped out of the ground,
fissures that went down to the molten core
(nickel, isn't it?) at the planet's center.
Old men tell little boys the local lore—
for instance, in this pond once a horse drowned,
crossing the ice too slowly one mild winter,
horse and sleigh, together. There was never a trace
of either. Deep? As the eyes in that boy's face.

It would be easy to imagine some kind of curse
on this deceptive pond, but it would be worse
to tell the truth, that this tranquility
is exactly what it seems. In the benign
water, horses, revolvers, beer cans wish
to intrude themselves, to take this landscape and sign
it, but they cannot. This silver civility,
like a queen's, distracts itself with little fish;
we can only presume upon it. Scrupulous, fair,
it shows us our own faces reflected there.

II

LUTE

*At Town Hall, in February, 1965, when Julian Bream came
out with a guitar for a second encore after a program of lute
and guitar music, members of the audience shouted, "Lute!
Lute!" Mr. Bream replied, "It's bad enough with six strings,
never mind fourteen."*

They are not serious, violins that sway
their hips and flash their naughty, varnished curves,
flirting with light. And lightly do they play.
Better the lute, whose music is the nerves
throbbing in pain and in key. The flesh on the string
pays for each note, as acupuncture scored
for lutenist and lute. In each cut chord,
each of them fights to make the other sing.

There are other cruel instruments. Flutes demand,
like adolescent girls, that drawn-out kiss.
But the lute, keening under the lutenist's hand,
big in the belly, wild and wanton, is
the hardest mistress. What hurt must go unheard
when, like the harpsichord's quills, on the lute's frets
bare fingers pluck out the music? And he gets
Cutting, Dowland, Batcheler, and Byrd.

His forehead furrows, eyebrows rise and fall.
Racked by the phrases, and in their sway, he sways.
The calluses of his long practice gall
as tender as in his first lute-playing days.
Pavane and galliard equally become
flowers he clutches closer to the thorn.
The lute plays only love songs. All songs torn
out of the body itself by its own thrum

are love songs, surely. Man and instrument
play off the painful comfort of keeping mute
against this playing of natural discontent
on the beautiful, globed body of the lute.
What woman can look and listen and not equate
herself with that shape he cradles. Gradually
she feels his pain, its strings, their harmony
in her stretched nerves, beginning to vibrate.

SWOBODA

*Wilhelm Kuhe "remembers that as a boy in Prague he met
Wenzel Swoboda, a double bass player, who had been a
member of the orchestra on the first night of* Don Giovanni *in
1787, conducted by Mozart himself."*

—PROGRAM NOTES TO *La Traviata*

Kuhe reports that Swoboda remembers . . .
but what could he remember? I have been
serif to the ELI's L, have marched,
strapped to the big, blue bulldog's thoompa-thoom,
and have heard the fweedle of the clarinets
dribbling down my ears. The trumpets' tune
was yards away, fluttering the flags
at the end of the bowl. We marched down the field
as letters we could not read, were ourselves the words.
And Swoboda heard nothing, and saw nothing,
remembered nothing but that his bow had moved
with a baton as twigs of the same tree
moving in a wind. What was there to tell
but his double bass's zormm-zormm-zormm?

LEPORELLO, IN HIS DRESSING ROOM

Il padron mio . . . but we never spoke Italian
or sang in Saltzburger harmonies. Don Juan
was Spanish, after all, a petty grandee
with a sallow complexion, too much grease in his hair,
and fatter than you'd imagine. His voice was deep,
not the rich basso you hear in your mind's ear,
but deep enough to be attractive to women—
many, but not that many. That thousand and three
he had in Spain couldn't have been six hundred,
which is still a lot, but beside the point. The numbers
are inflated because they are easy to understand.
He is remembered, but why he is remembered
has been forgotten. They make up all kinds of stories,
intricate seductions, changes of costume,
me, the lowly Leporello, singing
under the balcony to his direction,
which is closer, having to do with the style of the thing
but not yet it, not him, not what I remember.
Think of the end, the dead *commendatore*,
the statue come to dinner. God, I was scared,
and he was, too. He was. I could see him tremble,
but he would not repent, would not, wrenched himself loose
and lay on the floor, quivering in fear,
and still would not take any of it back.
You hear the shriek, which is neither Italian nor Spanish,
nor any other language, nor even music
except for the instruments running down the scale,
a pure shriek, as the devils carry him off,
and it stays with you in the taxi, all the way home.
It has stayed with me for years, in my ear, throat,
and I understand it: the cry of the faithful servant,
for he was a servant too, his own man,
serving his pleasure as I was serving him.
But he was more loyal than I, or any man,
and would not betray at the end that little master,
nor lose his honor just to keep his soul.

THE DEATH OF MOZART

Uraemia is painful enough without birds
chirping their heads off, warbling in thirds
while you're busy dying. A little quiet, please.
I want no canary around for my decease.
No more did he. But still, it is bothersome
to think that when his final hour had come
Mozart sent his canary away. Did the bird
make mistakes? sing badly what Mozart heard
in his mind's ear, following a score
of canary music? Or, did the bird soar
on aviary arias, a strain
so fine that he beat time with throbs of pain?
Or worse, did the bird's song suggest a measure
there was no more time for, now, so that the pleasure
of composing turned to the pain of holding a flood,
as the body held the urine in the blood?
I fear the worst, that Mozart, as you or I,
just wanted quiet, quiet in which to die,
unbroken by any sound but his own breath.
With the bird gone, he had quiet. Which was death.

THREE LOVE POEMS

1.
There is an eagle on the ash Yggdrasil
who knows many things,
but not you who are too quick for him,
too cunning.

Chen-kuan ended the hsiu-ts'ai degree,
so few could obtain it. But no hsiu-ts'ai
could read your moods,
know what to say to you.

Wife, I am dull of wit and thick of tongue.
What chance have I, what hope,
my love, but love of learning
at your hard school?

2.
I have watched you watch him, seen the dance
of your eyes to the hummingbird feet of the airborne Russian,
felt your pulse as the Italian tenor sang
trills on the vein in front of his forehead, and yours.

The dancer goes off with some boy, and the stout tenor
goes back to his countess, somewhere on Central Park South,
while we have coffee and walk five blocks to the car.

I will not tell you they are faithless gallants
while your ear still sings, your eye still dances, riding,
but know I am the danseur, lifting you up,
the tenor to your soprano. Hear my "Andiamo!"
a little above the speed limit, driving home.

3.
At absolute zero, time will freeze
because the air will freeze, and all the music
from transmitters will congeal, the notes slow,
falter, float like steelies. And words. And waves.
Emotion: so that the green of lust, and purple
of affection and orange aggressiveness will form
rainbows. Everything will be rock, crystal,
and there will be no vicissitudes

but only continual contemplation of
the moment before, with consciousness and conscience
solid, rock sure. Conditions of spirit
will shine like lavalieres, or not shine
like all the towering slag heaps of De Beers.
Meanwhile, on cold days, I love you more.

A COMPLIMENT UPON A LAUGH

FOR S. P. G.

Properly heard, it floats
from Catherine's window to break
on crusts of Kremlin snow
or across moats
of Henri's *grands chateaux.*
Oh, it should wake
the light along the royal air
ordered by *plantes jardinières!*
And such lewd laughter
should cheer the desperate throng
as if it were the rallying song
of their better hereafter.
The empress, the mistress, or the queen,
laughing that way, gay but obscene,
alerts the ministers at the fringes
of that fabric that she weaves
so carelessly (lighter than leaves
on one of their ruinous November binges).
And I have heard it from your throat
and offer roars of mobs you've never heard,
rioting out there, clamoring for the vote,
but ready to quiet at your word.
"Yes, they adore you.
There are millions, ma'am, out in the streets
loyal in their devotion for you.
I'd open the window but for the murderous heat . . ."
You smile and turn away.
                                    Include
all such histories, so gaudily true
in the tribute which is properly your due
for that improper laugh, so fine, so lewd.

TABLEAU A LA ROUSSEAU

That lions like lavender is amiable; for the mane's
tawny to find complement in the green
spike with the sharp accent of the blossom
is not mere whimsy, as delight in catnip
would be, but somehow right. One can nearly
see in those slow yellow eyes a need to express
the innate refinement lions have, and lavender
must be a relief from the flesh-red, blood-red
redness of their usual provender
and the bloody obviousness of crimson with gold.
Or, it may be the odor, or
just to adore such a vegetable vegetable.
It extends the range of lions, even as they
extend its possibilities: they may
love most to patronize, to let it be said
that among the lovers of lavender are lions.

SAPPHIC FRAGMENTS

Because of my pain she wrote.
The rest is gone.
Editors, blinder than Homer, fire,
water, rot, monks, the rotten
bishop, St. Gregory of Nazi
                        anzos,
mummy wrappers, perverse, preserved
only this. Imagine
                Because of
Achilles' wrath. . .
              Imagine the rest.
Her silence, the silence of women, fascinates.
It and her *Garlands of celery* makes
a mad scene, an entire *Hamlet* but
with men left out—Queen Gertrude and Ophelia.
'*We shall give,*' said the father could be her *Lear*.
But what of *As long as you wish*?
Who speaks, who sacrifices herself, and suffers until
Unexpectedly?
Everything is.
Even *The queenly dawn*. Everything
is unexpectedly because of her pain.

DIALOGUE IN ITHAKA

"Those impossible tales he tells Penelope . . ."
  "She believes him."
"And her story of the years she spent weaving. . ."
  "He believes her."
"You really think that they believe each other?"
  "Man, you'll believe anything!"

UPON RECEIVING A BOOK OF POEMS

For George Garrett

Your book is . . . But another friend was here
who'd brought a house gift for us, a crystal bowl,
a co-incidence, but our minds work that way,
and the world, as we have agreed, is a teaching machine.
It's a lovely bowl, clean of line, clear,
and catching the light live. When he'd left the room,
I did what we all do, sooner or later,
deliberately or just by accident,
and flicked my fingernail against its rim.
It's a good bowl, and the crystal rang and rang.
The sound of the glass was clear as its light and line.
And I have read your book, and flicked my nail
against its rim, and having done so, thank you,
for the air rings, sings with a clear tone.

Never mind well wrought urns, but consider this bowl,
and what it would be if it could never break
but go on ringing, as if God's own nail
had struck it. Books are like that sometimes. Yours is.

IMPROVISATION ON THEMES OF JOHN DONNE

We know that keening. What we do not know
is whether the comptroller is in a hurry, or Otto
Preminger is passing through, or the cops
are speeding after a speeding driver, or before
an ambulance, for a birth or a death. It stops

but we do not send to know for whom the siren
screams. It will be in the papers, tucked in with the foreign
exchange listings and port departures. It's not,
anyway, for us, except to wonder whether
it's car or driver or fire itself that's hot.

Those horsemen ride in style now—Cadillacs—
ambulances and hearses; or fire trucks
by La France, and the silver siren on the side.
Death is proud, an official who sometimes deigns
to take a lucky constituent for a ride.

EPITAPH FOR GOLIATH

After so many victories, one
defeat, and that one by a stone:
but let this stone atone for that
breach of the order of combat.
He was a victim of a ruse
of the rude boy of the barbarous Jews.
Goliath shall have honor while
men yet have any use for style
or the purity of form they mean
by the accolade of Philistine.

PROLEGOMENON TO THE STUDY OF POETICS

The population doubles itself and redoubles.
We are squeezing out the animals; the time will come
when we squeeze out one another. Minerals wash
into the oceans; the Atlantic and the Pacific
get to be more and more like the Dead Sea.
I understand the moon is getting closer,
will fall back, will kill us all one day.
I hear the clock tick and wait for silence.

Oh, but the poems! What about the poems?

The Greeks, the Jews, the Chinese have misled us.
Think, rather, of some exquisite Mayan
or of an Etruscan bard, or of all the minstrels
of cultures you and I have never heard of . . .
Try to imagine their intricate lyrics, praising
the beauty of the moon, of the sea, of love.

GREAT CIRCLE ROUTE

And North means to all: "Reject."

Across the St. Lawrence and on to the brownish gray
of Newfoundland at five hundred miles an hour.
Below there was neither road nor water tower
but only the geese of the map—Gander, Goose Bay—
and the shadows of planes like ours that flitted over
endless scrub. They served cocktails and we
stared down, amused, trying to discover
some sign of habitation, but could see

nothing. It got dark. We ate and slept
and forgot it, but in the cities it came back
as something we'd left behind. Your gloves? You wore.
My sunglasses? I had them. But we kept
looking for something or other, having lost track
of that glimpse of tracklessness of Labrador.

CASTELLO SFORZESCO

That pigeon up in the arrow slit! The bird
is mocking. How else explain the gentle dove
positioned thus upon a bartizan?
We lay our siege to it, for we have heard
about walls and the something there is that doesn't love
them. Perhaps it hasn't reached Milan,

or the something that does is stronger here,
the fascination with merlons and crenelles,
with turrets, quoins, corbels, machicolation.
Across the moat, the looming of the sheer
curtain wall invites the mangonels
and battering rams of our imagination.

We have never been bombed back home, and the civil war
soldiers are green with age in our green squares.
Our children climb on those cannon balls piled in
pyramids. But a fort, picked up off the floor
of a child's room, inflated as in nightmares,
amplifies the message: We have soft skin,

and we want metal armor, rock walls, want
shells for our innocence. Admit the neighbor
was not all wrong about good fences. Those
running cairns that criss-cross all Vermont
were meant to be there, cost the farmer labor,
as he cleared his fields and piled the stones in rows.

It was never just the wanderlust of cattle
he built against, but an enemy. The frost
heaves the ground. The walls fall down again,
and in the spring he mends them, doing battle
with the weight of the stones themselves. The fight is lost
eventually; stones sit on the graves of men

and always win in the end. But in the meantime
let us admire the will that builds a wall,
the claim, the honor. The stone put upon stone
is something the enemy will have to climb
or batter down, a postponement at least. These tall
parapets challenge us all to look to our own.

BATH

On the one side, cliffs and a slope down to the river,
placid even above its gentle falls
along the parade garden and colonnade
where swans swim and flowers bloom in November,
and then, on the rise, Squire Allworthy's houses,
the Circus, the Crescents: Bath is a fine town.
But clear away the houses, clear away
the ruins of the baths, the baths themselves,
back to the first mud hole and to Bladud,
the swineherd prince of Cornwall, leprous, banished,
who wallowed like his pigs in this hot mud
and was cured by the mud or sulphur or miracle.
He lived, returned to reign and had an heir.
At these white bones of fascinating fact
Bladud wondered, as at his own, whole flesh,
which he pinched white to watch it turn dream pink,
and each time more amazed, and each new day
a gift, a miracle. He decided that.
The cure was miraculous, or, if natural,
the finding of the spring was miraculous,
and Bladud in that wild west spoke of ease,
the smooth agreement of rough rock and sea,
pink dawns that end the blackest howling night,
and found in every harshness something mild.
He was a despot of benevolence,
a mystic, and to study nature right,
Bladud, in the fullness of his age,
healed and holy, reverend Cornish king,
resigned throne, sceptre, crown to his son, Leir,
and went to Trinovantum to try again
to fly on the wings of Icarus. Magic, but magic
is making miracles, and Bladud studied magic,
and did rise up a little, high enough
to fall and break that skin he had thought sacred.
The secular bone broke, blood ran, brain splashed
upon Apollo's roof. The sins of fathers
are easier to bear than a father's grace.
And Leir believed his father. His life, too,
he owed to that hot spring that bubbled free
even in winters when the river froze.
It was, his father was, he had to be
exceptional, and therefore he was kind,

a good king, a good father, a good man.
Why not, then, in old age, resign the throne?
Why not believe his daughter Goneril?
Why doubt Cordelia's reticence? Belief,
the moral ether Leir flew through, was higher,
thinner than Trinovantum's air. Bladud
was right about the growling of the sea,
and the wind that cracks its cheeks. They are gentle,
gentler than speeches daughters make.
So Leir fell too.

     Still, in the Pump Room,
the water from the old spring splashes up,
greenish inside a great glass bowl, and tourists
queue to taste the famous curative.
A string ensemble plays. One takes a glass,
catches a tumblerful from one of the spigots,
and tries a sip from Bladud's ancient mud hole.
But people are sensible. Nobody drains the glass.
Whatever the water's power, it is bitter.

HELLBRUNN

FOR J. K.

It isn't, but we think of Tivoli
and d'Este's fountains and the way his villa
sits on the hill, commands the waterfall
pouring those millions and millions of gallons down
to slake Lucrezia's little boy's ennui
with the gush of the water organ or the dribble
from shell to shell down the sides of the staircase
that visitors used to climb and tourists still
brave the warnings of the guides to try
weak hearts against Ippolito's hauteur.

It isn't Tivoli. This Sitticus
worked water too, and poured pride on his callers
but with jets in the walls, with fun-house waterspouts
up from the floors, down from the stag horn sprays,
bum-wetting bishops, head-soaking Salzburg burghers
he lured like fish into his grotto nets
of nonsensical bird-noise machines, which water
obscurely ran. Or from the outdoor benches
the fountains now spurt ten feet up in the air
which used to goose his dinner guests who sat
still until he moved, bidet buffoon,
jet jester, and His Eminence, Archbishop.

They meet somewhere. These waggish waterworks
flow into the Salzach and into the sea,
as those so stately fountains fall again
and, slowing through the intricate sluices, flow
back into Tivoli's river, and on to the Tiber
which also finds the sea. These fountaineers
were not so far apart. Sitticus' bubble,
designed to keep cut flowers fresh three weeks,
would have delighted d'Este, whose twin mermaids,
their nipples spouting, return the fancied favor.
To disapprove is difficult. That face,
even that foolish face with the running water
inside the head somewhere, filling a cup
and tripping a balance to make the eyes roll back
and tongue stick out in that most common insult,
commands affection—that any man could labor
and lavish love on trivial tricks like this—
and hypnotizes: we listen for the splash,

wait for the awful tongue to repeat its insult,
master the mechanism and learn the rhythm,
to feel the flow of water as a pulse.

This vulgar Sitticus knew the medium,
the water he wrote his name on; the cascade
of questionable jokes must lose their point.
The d'Este crest of eagles and fleurs de lis,
worked in stone, is worn away by the water.
Even the finest fountains are temporary.
The splendid spray falls back in self-abuse
to grind the cupidons, the nymphs, the dolphins
smooth again, faceless, nameless, blank as water.
The worst outrages then, for obliteration
must gradually improve the whole effect,
as, here, at Hellbrunn, where the only insult
is in the water, softening the rage
a dead man felt, and we come to feel, drowning.

A RONDELET FROM A FRAGMENT OF ARCHILOCHUS

The sea heaves.
Glaukos, look how in its bed
the sea heaves.
Over the Gyrean cape, the cloud leaves
a stain that spreads, turns blue to lead:
a storm is coming. And in its dread
the sea heaves.

A TRIOLET FROM ANOTHER FRAGMENT

I lie, sick with desire,
with love gnawing my bones'
marrow. On my bed's pyre,
I lie, sick with desire,
feeling the gods' ire
they dispense from their cool thrones.
I lie, sick with desire,
with love gnawing my bones.

GALLUS

(After Ecloga X)

"That greedy goat munches like a machine,
leaves, more leaves, whole hillsides of leaves,
and look at the endless lurching of the bee
from clover blossom to clover blossom, obscene,
insatiate. Even the grass here lives,
soaking, sucking the rainclouds' udders dry.
And will you, Gallus, with your trickle of tears,
surfeit the even greater appetite
of the god of love for pain?"
                              By a gray boulder,
Gallus answered, spoke of wild boars, bears,
of the hard life, camp on hard ground at night,
frost and its numb relief as it gets colder . . .

Cytheris had run off. His darling actress
was doing the act with Antony now, and Gallus,
the elegant poet, the intelligent soldier, lay
on the ground, reduced to an ooze of moans, sighs,
tears, sweat, because the seed in him was
curdling in its sack for that stupid slot.
What could I do but cajole, jolly, bully,
try to divert him with whores, long walks, poems,
and talk of poems. It did no good. He went
to fight at Actium, at Paraetonium
(whipped Antony twice), and to fight at Thebes.

In pride he carved his name on the pyramids,
and Augustus called him home, because of his pride.
Gaul, claiming his victories? Not for himself,
but for the old score, for his Cytheris—
of whom the Senate neither knew nor cared.
Disgraced, he killed himself, as Antony
killed himself. It comes to that too often.
Too often, my friend, and I grieve for you. Often.

"Tree nymphs no longer please me. Never mind
nymphs, the trees themselves have blurred
to brown boredom, sticks stuck in the dirt.
Wilderness is tame. I've seen the blind
snowstorms of Macedon, been in absurd

swelter of deserts, frozen, baked the hurt,
but have it still."
                    Thus would Gallus say,
and I should have to agree. "Let's go then, friend.
This shade is bad for poetry. Our throats
are dry. Let's go home." In such a way,
I'd bring the pastoral to its natural end.
We could go together, herding the fucking goats.

III

ANOTHER LETTER TO LORD BYRON

Everyone gets junk mail, a bill, a notice
    of a private sale, an alumni fund appeal,
letters from strangers . . . The one that Auden wrote is
    one of these, though clever enough. Did you feel
the eight krona stamp redeemed it? That's ten zlotys,
    or about a hundred lire—not a great deal,
but the names of the coins are diverting. Or possibly you
collect postage stamps? It's something to do.

It must be dull to be dead. You can't write,
    or, if you do, you can't send it off to the printer
the way you used to. So a letter might
    have been fun to get. Did you spend the winter
feeling the envelope, holding it up to the light,
    and wondering whom you knew in such a hinter-
land as Iceland? I know it would pique
my interest to get mail from Reykjavik.

Harwich is less impressive, surely, than is
    Reykjavik. But when I go to post
my letter, I may do so from Hyannis,
    which is more amusing. Or there are a host
of towns named after you. The one in Maine is
    closest, but you have a wandering ghost—
which is fitting. There's a Byron or Byronville
in Okla., Wyo., Calif., Minn., and Ill.

But never mind. The postmark's hardly crucial.
    The main thing is that after thirty years
another letter that's addressed to you shall
    seem, I trust, no great intrusion. There's
lots that's happened, though I hope the news shall
    not depress you. Three decades of wars,
and the prospect of a future about which it's said
that those who are left alive will envy the dead.

But politics is not at all my metier.
    You took it up at the end, I know, but I
find it vicious enough, if rather petty (a
    moral hedging), to deal with the canaille

of publishers, editors, agents. Those *diavoletti!* (Eh?
   That's nearly impossible to justify.
But then I've just been to Venice, and saw your palazzo.
   Is that enough excuse to polyglot so?)

I've changed the subject sooner than I'd intended,
   but as long as I'm on the new one, literature
is just as much a mess as ever—splendid
   livings for lousy authors, and good books fewer
and farther than ever between . . . But then, when did
   it ever appear to be better or different? You are
a perfect example of what can happen when
a poet is taken up by other men,

to be praised or damned. The public is mostly jerks.
   The common reader is common, and to hell
with him and with critics, trading in smiles and smirks,
   and making careers for themselves with their swell
Collected Essays more in mind than the works
   in hand. Even you're not doing too well.
I mention the disrepair of your reputation
only to demonstrate that of our situation.

No one reads poetry anyway now, except
   other poets—which is quite distressing.
They cannot be much as readers, being inept
   as rhymers (those that can rhyme), while confessing
to mental illness, or listing girls they've slept
   with (those that like girls) . . . But I am digressing.
In a time of tastelessness and epic slaughter,
we need some of your hock and soda water.

Not that it's all that bad. There is some verse
   well wrought. One can get in an age of iron
good iron work sometimes. A pigskin purse
   can be made of a sow's ear. One may not expire on
the beauty of it, but one could do worse.
   The manipulation of language . . . But, Lord Byron,
I scarcely need tell you. Your magnificent feminine
rhymes are more than fun for apothegming in.

They show contempt for the worst kind of good taste,
   and for readers—most of the few—who save up snatches

to make a mental sampler of, the paste
   pot minds of crack-pots. And the catch is
that by the way you sneer at the half-caste
   intellectuals who can't tell dispatches
of the AP from poems, look for meanings,
and of course miss all the point in their dull gleanings.

I hadn't meant to go on so. Do excuse
   my grumbling. I know it's rather foolish,
but I've been depressed lately. All the news
   is bad; the weather's damp and has turned coolish;
my mood's dark, the color of a bruise.
   And I've been bothered by the very ghoulish
notion that the books around me may
come to life and attack me any day.

Or not the books, but their authors, all the dead
   giants of letters whom time has not quite hushed.
It'd be delightful except that they have shed
   their skins, their flesh, their bones, and are all crushed
to disembodied voices, dull as lead.
   I have the feeling that I am ambushed
by the naked ones who have shown up to haunt
me. But I can't imagine what they want.

I shouldn't like to think it's vampirism,
   nor envy, nor contempt. Perhaps they warn
that poetry is light spread through a prism,
   and suddenly, on some innocuous morn
the prism breaks, and the recidivism
   is to the whiteness from which it was born—
no rhetoric, no images, no sound,
just volumes of blank pages, buckram bound.

Or they sing, hey-diddle, the cat and the fiddle—but
   even its nine lives prove to be finite,
and after performing on lengths of its own gut,
   it dies and the music dies. There's a moral in it.
I'm sure there is. I can't tell you just what,
   but I'm sure I'll think of something. Give me a minute.
Art is odd. Consider the dog and how
he laughed to see the hell scared out of the cow.

Well, here I am, half-dog, half-cow, half-cat
   (that's too many halves by half). All right, half-wit,
fooling around as you did once. But that
   is greatly comforting: in the little skit
from the Nightmare Follies—now in its fifth week at
   my local, mental theater—you're a big hit.
Among those shades, you shine, and my attention all
focuses on you, who are three dimensional.

You come through whole, and live, and are not merely
   a name on the spine of your book and its index card.
The gestures you make in your poems, the jokes, are clearly
   those of a man who's trying very hard
—and willing to pay the price, even pay dearly—
   not only not to be boring, but not to be bored
himself. Yourself. Myself. I know how it is.
It's always tough in the Quality Lit. Biz.

Therefore, my letter. Partly to let you know
   that you're still alive and well, which pleases me
as much as it pleases you, and to say hello.
   With any luck, in two thousand and three,
somebody else will drop you a line, and so
   keep the game going. Auden, I, he
thank you for teaching how to play it coolly.
It is, as I am, sir, yours, very truly.

IV

EXHORTATION TO AN ARAB FRIEND (1965)

At the Pond of Humm, Mohammed named the treasures:
The Book of God, the People, the Household.
Belief must have, as vessel, the believers,
and therefore al-Islam; and God must have
perfection of His pleasure and His will,
His word proclaimed, obeyed, made history,
and therefore tribal pride is sanctified,
and Khalid strikes at Ctesiphon and Merv
as Joshua struck at Jericho. War becomes
jihad, and the pride of blood is a pool of blood
of which a hundredth part would flood the Humm.
So Persia fell to Khalid, and Egypt fell
to Amr, who sent the news back to Umar:
"I shall not describe the city I have captured.
Suffice it to say I have counted four thousand villas,
four thousand baths, four hundred palaces."
Umar gave the messenger bread and dates,
and thanks and praise to God, Alahu akbar!
for the city of Alexander.
                              All of us prosper.
We build our cities of marble, our cities of gold,
and say of Babylon or Athens or Rome
that surely such splendor must meet with the favor of God,
must prove that favor. Snuggled in His will,
we stride the high towers, but towers fall.
Even Jerusalem fell, our beautiful city,
Solomon's city, Solomon's temple, all
toys of fortune. And you build Baghdad,
three walls, four gates, and the green dome at the hub,
to do the word of God in your round city.
You prospered there, as all the nations once
have prospered, early or late. Your soldiers learned
that camphor was not salt to be used in cooking.
They had never before seen gold, changed gold dinars
for silver dirhams.
                              We, too, tended sheep,
saw God, and made a kingdom, and we knew
what you were thinking—that there is no other greatness
than God's alone. But heaven is more splendid
than our Jerusalem or your Baghdad.

The glory of those cities was merely our own.
Of the 22,000 rugs of the just Haroun,
count one for prayer, the rest for luxury,
and reckon the cost as you learned the comforts of Persia
and made the clear horizon of the faith
shimmer as through the heat waves in the desert.
The cause became the excuse; in the bazaars
there were spices from India, Malay dies and metals,
honey and fur from Norway, and ivory
and slaves from Africa. Chinoiserie
was fashionable in Baghdad. The excuse
became a pretext.

                        Declare Alahu akbar!
God is great! even when Mongols come
and Holagou Khan, the grandson of Zingis,
stands at the triple wall of the round city.

Mostosem comes out from his harem of seven hundred
to declare that divine decree has raised the throne
of the Abbassid Caliphate. And God is great!
still while the Khan lays siege to the city and storms it,
burns it and rakes its ashes. Islam fell back
to the desert, the hot sun of the true faith.
You learned what we had learned of God and greatness.

And again. There was snow on the ground for a hundred days
before Constantinople, and the earth
froze hard as rock, the rock as cold as metal.
Suliman was dead of indigestion
having eaten at a single meal a kid,
six roasted fowls, seventy pomegranates,
and a prodigy of the grapes of Taref. Dead
and of no help. Omar ben Abdalaziz
succeeded, prayed, was not to be disturbed,
and by his silence was the siege continued.
From the air, Greek fire, Medea's fire, fell
to sear the snow to steam, to boil the bay,
and all were lost of eighteen hundred ships.
In the spring, in a second wave, seven hundred sixty
set out for Constantinople. Five returned.
Among the losses, count the old idea
that through Islam the world would be perfected,

and the pleasure of Allah be done on earth.
That pleasure was defeat, and at Toulouse,
your Zama lost to the Duke of Aquitaine
his life, his army, providence. I know
the shine of dawn, the gray wolf tail in the east
that sweeps the sky, that burnishes to gold,
and in our dawn we lived in God's hand, too,
with miracles, miracles pouring down from heaven.
The burden of that old prosperity
is the memory we keep, that it keep us.

Nothing but from us. The Ifranji knows
nothing of our lightness of breath, the brightness
of our sky, the glare of white sun on our rocks
in the dry air. In the hot, dry wind, the Samun,
the living God has shown Himself like fire,
has revealed to the two of us, who have taught them—
religion as well as poetry, medicine,
philosophy, numbers, and all manner of knowledge,
but not the knowledge written upon our faces,
running in lines from the eyes, in wadis of wisdom,
graven in flesh by light. It was in the desert,
where we looked for water, for dates to keep alive,
He showed Himself to our prophets and to us.
In the light of reason, in the light of our blood kinship,
in the light of that desert sun that made us both,
let us remember Quedubah, how we lived,
the two of us, greatly, in Cordova, in Baghdad,
and in Damascus, and have converse again:
of death, first, the subject at Almagor,
where riflemen, yours and ours, confront each other
across the river. Death, except as a test
of nerve or faith is not interesting.
We both know that, having lost all count of our dead.
The Greeks, the Romans choked upon our dead.
The Franks hurled themselves upon you, and your dead
were like a wall before Gerusalemme.
There is faith enough to finish us both. We have swarmed
the earth, have died like flies. Exiles or rulers,
it makes no difference. But coming back here, now,
after all those years, should Ishmael and Isaac
repeat, complete, what Cain and Abel started?

JONAH: A REPORT

He is mad. He is filthy. He sits all day in his shack.
He says he never sleeps and never wakes,
but hangs between in a trance. His hair is white
and yet we know his age is thirty-one.
The cures are remarkable. Of course, the doctors
say he is a fake, but cannot explain
the cases, scores of them, hundreds, of small children
sick to death with fever and brought to him
at the last moment, when all other hope is lost,
and suddenly well again. And deaf made to hear
and blind to see again. The usual things.

The dream, however, is dangerous. He says
that all his powers came to him in the dream,
and he tells the dream, over and over again.
We have asked him, we have begged him to desist,
but still he tells his dream, this blasphemous dream,
which threatens our religion and our people.

The Dream
"I lay three days. The coffinmaker came
to make my coffin, but while he worked the wood,
I heard my sickness speak to me. It promised
that from the Lord of the Ocean I might receive
the gift of healing. Therefore I asked my father
to let my body be buried at once, in the sea.
    "They carried me to the harbour and found a ship
ready to set sail, and loaded me on.
My sickness churned the sea, and the mariners
threw me over the side and sailed away
I fell upon the ocean in my coffin,
and the coffin was a boat which bore me, swifter
than any ship. I came, then, to an island
where the Lady of the Ocean makes her home.
Naked, she welcomed me, and gave me her teat
and suckled me, and sang to me of hardships,
of the trouble I should find, and the weariness.
I laid my head in her lap and slept a while.
    "When I woke, alone, to the rushing of wings,
I saw a bird like an eagle, but larger, larger,

with feathers of iron and beak of blackest stone.
The eagle plucked me up and carried me
to the top of a mountain. There a birch tree grew,
and the Lord of the Tree bade me break a branch,
but when I touched the tree, it groaned and cried.
I broke a twig, the smallest I could find,
and felt the pain of it in my little finger,
which also broke, but when I touched the twig
to the broken finger, it healed me instantly.
The Lord of the Tree approved and told me his secrets,
the seven virtues of the seven plants,
the powers of nine stones and of nine metals.

    "I visited the tents of illness, torn,
and in a barren place. In the first tent, Syphilis
tore out my living heart. In the next, Madness
cut off my head. Leprosy peeled my skin,
and the others took my nerves, my bones, my blood.
But the eagle, who is Lord of the Sky, returned
and carried my body's pieces to a cave
where a smith with one eye beat upon an anvil
and forged me whole again. I was molten hot
and he threw me down to cool in a deep pool.

    "The pool was a part of the ocean, very deep
where all the oceans meet. The Lord of the Ocean
sulks there, in his castle. He was the Lord
of Chaos before our God created the world
and separated dry land from the water.
The Lord of the Ocean is angry, and sends the waves
to beat upon the land and wash it away,
and sends the storms to sink the ships of land
that sail upon his sea, and sends the wind
to blow down trees that men build into ships.
He fought with me and killed me many times,
but every time I lived again, and was stronger,
for the smith had forged me well. The Lord of the Ocean
at last relented and offered me his daughter,
an ugly hag with green snakes for her hair,
scales for skin, sea scallops for dugs.
I lay with her (and still I stink of fish)
and she told me her father's secrets—of the waters,
fresh and salt, and all the sacred springs,
and how to find the water when digging wells.

Then she put me inside an enormous fish
which brought me back to earth and Nineveh."

He does not insist, of course, on the literal truth
of everything in the dream, but he does repeat it,
and the people, because he cures their children, believe.
The man is remarkable, but Israel
cannot survive his kindnesses. Therefore,
the committee on heterodoxy recommends
that Jonah be stoned to death, as the law prescribes,
but privately, and at night. In a few years
if he is not forgotten, let us publish
our own, official account of his exploits.
We can make him a minor prophet, let him go
on a voyage, even let him get thrown in the sea,
and on his return he can preach something inoffensive—
virtue and reform are the usual things.
This is our report and our proposal,
submitted on the fifteenth day of Adar,
in the year 3436 of the Lord's people.

THE COVENANT

Let the world be wary of my son,
be gentle with him, be reverent—
not for the laughter I love,
nor for his possible Hamlet or Zauberflöte,
but as their very savior
                         from those glaciers
the ovens turned to slush, from the clouds
that gathered above those chimneys.
Let the world rejoice in him,
its trustee and its signator
whose person is as holy as a king's,
the child-hero, Dutchboy of the dikes:
he keeps the ice caps frozen, the salt sea
splashing in its bed, the clouds moving,
the world safe, at least for another lifetime,
safe, at least for a while, at least from the flood.

PROLOGUE TO A PLAY: SAMUEL SPEAKS

The miraculous days are over. Now there is no
belief or disbelief but something half-way,
half-hearted. The conscript army parades and the people
cheer, but it is a vain hope and has no object.
They wait for another miracle, but have forgotten
what they are waiting for, that they wait at all.
Even the very old can hardly remember
stories they heard in childhood: of crossing the desert,
water gushing from the struck rock, food
falling from the sky, the sea parting.
Not even the children now accept such tales.
The state therefore was necessary for endurance,
the freshness of love having somehow run dry.
And now will a man love his wife by the state's contract
and father will feed his son by the state's law,
and widow will have the farm by law, for we
who lived freely in our Father's house have demanded
a lease to our own room as between strangers.
By politics do all men become strangers,
to be dealt with as strangers. With the state will no man feed
the wanderer, with the state will no man repair
the road in front of his house. With the state no man
will teach his own child, for the state will do, compel
these things as if no virtue were in the world.
Not to the horizon, but the boundary,
not to the hilltop but the flag will men look,
and the king will rule as if there were no God.
And love with nothing to do will be sentiment,
and God with nothing to do will be an idea.
This, and more, I said, but the soul's cowardice,
which is fear of anarchy, could not be driven out.
The people demanded, and, therefore, I annointed
Saul, a common man, and made him king.

A GARLAND FOR ST. AGNES ON MY BIRTHDAY

The war goes on. The seven virtues strive
still with the seven sins, but to no conclusion,
in obscure parts of the world where hills' and rivers'
and generalissimos' names are hard to remember,
barbarous and absurd. Elsewhere, the virtues
triumphant and serene arrange themselves
in various coalitions to meet the occasions
of architecture—seven or ten or four,
like parties in Italian cabinets.
But buildings have four walls and naves four vaults
more often than not, and therefore Agnes, Barbara,
Catherine, and Margaret stand in a line together,
representing the triumphs of innocence, of faith,
of intellectual, and of artistic devotion.

I have no saints, but came into the world
under the sign of St. Agnes Hospital
whose triumph over innocence mother feared,
a popish plot to baptize sickly babies.
I thrived, however, and on the eighth day
was circumcised, according to ritual,
mine, and in her hospital. Triumphant,
I hold no grudge against Agnes—her idea,
and what else is she now but an idea,
a floating allegory turned to legend?
To watch and fast on Agnes' eve may hint
husbands in dreams of "azure lidded sleep,
in blanchèd linen, smooth and lavender'd,"
to pray nine times to the moon and fast three times
on three St. Agnes eves, catch any man.
It has nothing to do with the actual little martyr
who appeared before her parents from the grave,
radiant in glory. An Hebrew Jew,
but how can I not be touched. Even the lamb
was added later: Agnes and agnus.
She can have a flock of lambs. And on her day
two lambs are brought to the pope and blessed and shorn
and their wool spun and woven by the sisters
into palls for the primates. Still, my Agnes
can have her pets, her primates and her pope,
but let her keep the *agnus castus*, too,

the twigs Greek matrons strewed their couches with
to celebrate Demeter's festival.
Like Agnes in her catacomb, Proserpine
appeared again, from under the earth. For the dead
to live again, if only in memory,
I'd pray to Agnes, claim her, yield to her.

Italian planes strafed Ethiopian camels
when I was born. The next year Spain began.
I was nearly four when Barcelona fell,
and four and a half when Warsaw was blitzkreiged.
In Sant' Agnese, built by Constantine,
an old mosaic shows her driven by soldiers,
presumably to the place of her death. My time
is Agnes' time. I have seen the pictures
of dead men on the ground, of women weeping
in streets over their corpses, and under the bombs
that still fell.
       I am nervous with Margaret's faith.
Her pearl, her *gran Margherita,* is the moon,
the gates of heaven, another world: fanatic.
Catherine, intellectual, with her wheel,
and translation to my Sinai, sets me off;
and a *Santa Caterina* is a mantis
and also an old maid on the skinny side.
I am fond of Barbara, the Heliopolitan
to whom was revealed the truth: that a bathroom
should be built with three windows rather than two
in honor of the Trinity. Her father
beheaded her at once with his own two hands,
and was struck down on the spot by thunder and lightning.
Barbara is the architects' patroness,
also of engineers, and protectress from thunder,
and from the lesser thunder, artillery.
I like the fine arts, fear the bombs and shells,
rockets and missiles, and well could warm to her
except for all those others, dead in my time,
not architects nor painters, and not poets
nor anything but millions and innocent.

It is thirty years my name has been in the files
of St. Agnes Hospital, White Plains, N.Y.,